For Gordon,
with whom I share the gift of marriage,
with much love

THE GIFT OF MARRIAGE

Written and compiled by Marion Stroud
Produced in conjunction with Pictor International

1817

HARPER & ROW, PUBLISHERS, SAN FRANCISCO

Cambridge, Hagerstown, New York, Philadelphia,
London, Mexico City, São Paulo, Sydney

FIRST U.S. EDITION

Acknowledgements
All pictures supplied by Pictor International,
24/32 Kilburn High Road, London NW6, England.

Bible quotations as follows: Genesis 2:18 ('Together'), Mark 10:5–8 ('The mystery of
marriage'), 1 Corinthians 13:4–7 and 1 John 4:19 ('Love: a way of life'), Proverbs
5:15,18–19 ('On being a husband'), Proverbs 12:4 ('On being a wife'), Song of Songs
4:12 ('A walled garden') from *Good News Bible*, copyright 1966, 1971 and 1976 American
Bible Society, published by Bible Societies/Collins; Ephesians 4:2,26,31–32 ('Forgive
and forget'), Ephesians 5:25,28–30,33 ('On being a husband'), Proverbs 31:10–12,25–26
and 1 Peter 3:1a,3–4 ('On being a wife') from *The Living Bible*, copyright 1971 Tyndale
House Publishers.

Extracts from The Marriage Service of *The Alternative Service Book 1980* are reproduced
by permission of the Central Board of Finance of the Church of England.
Other copyright material as follows: 'All he ever dreamed' from Ruth Bell Graham,
Sitting by My Laughing Fire, copyright © 1977 by Ruth Bell Graham, used by permission
of Word Books, Publisher, Waco, Texas; 'I choose you' adapted from 'Wedding by the
sea' in *A touch of wonder* by Arthur Gordon, copyright © 1974 by Fleming H. Revell
Company; 'A growing love' and 'Thank you' from *A growing love*, copyright © 1977
Ulrich Schaffer, published by Harper & Row; 'A psalm for marriage' and 'The good
days of marriage' from *I've got to talk to somebody, God* © 1968, 1969 by Marjorie Holmes
Mighell, reprinted by permission of Doubleday and Company, Inc. Extracts by Walter
Trobisch are taken from *I Married You*, copyright © 1971 Walter Trobisch, published by
Inter-Varsity Press, Downers Grove, Illinois.

Every effort has been made to trace and contact copyright owners. If there are any
inadvertent omissions in the acknowledgements, we apologize to those concerned.

Printed in Italy by New Interlitho S.P.A., Milan.

Library of Congress Cataloging in Publication Data
Stroud, Marion.
    THE GIFT OF MARRIAGE.

    1. Marriage—Addresses, essays, lectures.   I. Title.
HQ734.S974 1982   306.8   81–48215
ISBN 0–06–067753–8   AACR2

82 83 84 85 86 10 9 8 7 6 5 4 3 2 1

A marriage. . .
makes of two fractional lives
a whole;
it gives to two purposeless lives
a work, and doubles the strength
of each to perform it;
it gives to two
questioning natures
a reason for living,
and something to live for;
it will give a new gladness
to the sunshine,
a new fragrance to the flowers,
a new beauty to the earth,
and a new mystery to life.

Mark Twain

TOGETHER

The Lord God said,
'It is not good for the man to live alone.
I will make a suitable companion
to help him.'

The Book of Genesis

Marriage is given,
that husband and wife may comfort and
help each other,
living faithfully together
in need and in plenty,
in sorrow and in joy.
It is given,
that with delight and tenderness
they may know each other in love,
and, through the joy of their bodily union,
may strengthen the union
of their hearts and lives.

The Marriage Service

MARRIAGE IS...

Marriage is a dynamic process of discovery.

Marriage is a journey, not an arrival.

In marriage, being the right person is as important as finding the right person.

Marriage is starting to love, over and over again.

Marriage is a life's work.

Marriage is an art. . .and like any creative process, it requires active thought and effort. We have to learn how to share on many different levels. We need to practise talking from the heart, and understanding attitudes as well as words. Giving generously and receiving graciously are talents that are available to anyone. But all these skills need to be developed, if the marriage picture that we paint is to be anything approaching the masterpiece that God intended.

A MEDITATION

'After the wedding reception, the couple left for an unknown destination.'

The church is empty now. The last flower has been coaxed into place; the clutter of leaves and florist's wire has gone; the rehearsal for tomorrow's ceremony is over, and for a few moments I can be alone.

Lord God, you know that we have looked forward to our wedding day for so long. Dreamed about it; saved for it; planned its every detail. But suddenly, amidst all the love and laughter and excitement, there is an insistent stirring of something else. Am I afraid? Or is it just that hollow feeling which comes when I face anything new. . .new people, a new job, or even waiting for midnight to chime and a new year to begin!

But this is much more than a new year. We shall leave our wedding reception, not for a secret honeymoon destination—like that couple mentioned in the newspaper last week—but for a journey into a whole new way of life! And how can we know where that journey will take us? Many marriages start off with such love and high hopes for the future, and still dwindle into boredom or worse. Yet no one gets married with the intention of being unhappy. We want to make our marriage work. But perhaps we shall need some help in order to live happily ever after. So if marriage really is a gift from you, God, please show us the right paths to take, and come with us on our journey.

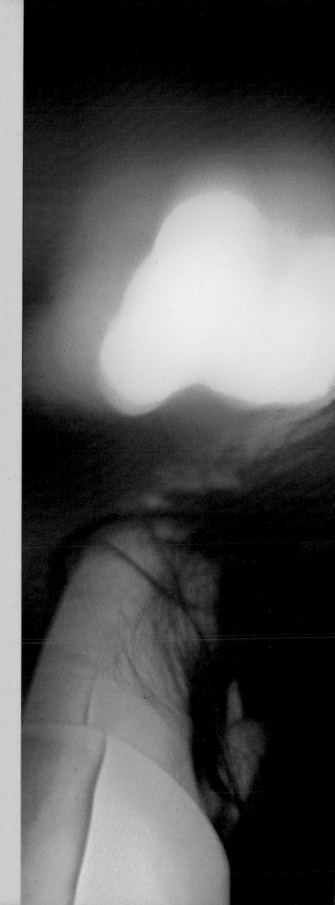

ALL
HE
EVER
DREAMED

God,
let me be all he ever dreamed
of loveliness and laughter.
Veil his eyes a bit
because
there are so many little flaws;
somehow, God,
please let him see
only the bride I long to be,
remembering ever after—
I was all he ever dreamed
of loveliness and laughter.

Ruth Bell Graham

I CHOOSE YOU

'I take you. . .to have and to hold, for better, for worse, for richer, for poorer, in sickness and in health. . .'

'These two have come here,' he said, 'to promise to face the future together, accepting whatever joy or sadness may lie ahead. . .Nothing is easier than saying words. Nothing is harder than living them day after day. What you promise today must be renewed and redecided tomorrow and each day that stretches out before you. At the end of this ceremony, legally you will be man and wife, but still you must decide each day that you want to be married.'

'Will you take this woman to be your wife?' the minister asked. 'Will you love and respect her? Will you be honest with her always? Will you stand by her through whatever may come? Will you make whatever adjustments are necessary so that you can genuinely share your life with her?' 'I will,' said the boy, and to the same questions the girl gave the same answer. 'I give you this ring,' the boy said. 'Wear it with love and joy. I *choose* you to be my wife, this day and every day.' 'I accept this ring,' she replied. 'I will wear it with love and joy. I *choose* you to be my husband this day and every day.'

'I take you. . .to love and to cherish. With my body I honor you. All that I am, I give to you. All that I have, I share with you, within the love of God.'

Love is not the feeling of a moment, but the conscious decision for a way of life.

THE MYSTERY

No man is an island, entire of itself; every
man is a piece of the Continent,
a part of the main.

John Donne

Jesus said, '. . .In the beginning, at the time
of creation, "God made them male and
female," as the scripture says. "And for
this reason a man will leave his father and
mother and unite with his wife, and the
two will become one." So they are no
longer two, but one.'

Mark's Gospel

OF MARRIAGE

'To become one flesh'...means that two persons share everything they have, not only their bodies, not only their material possessions, but also their thinking and their feeling, their joy and their suffering, their hopes and their fears, their successes and their failures. 'To become one flesh' means that two persons become completely one with body, soul, and spirit and yet there remain two different persons. This is the innermost mystery of marriage. It is hard to understand. Maybe we can't understand it at all. We can only experience it.

Walter Trobisch

A GIFT OF GOD

The Scriptures teach us
that marriage is a gift of God...
a holy mystery
in which man and woman
become one flesh.

The Marriage Service

It's all very well for them to say that it's in
the Bible, but what did God mean by it?
How can two people become one person?
The joining of our bodies in physical love
produces a fleeting oneness—and that can
be fantastic. But most of the time we are
just two people who love one another, but
are so very different. We have different
jobs, different likes and dislikes, different
abilities and very different ways of doing
things.

So if we are to be 'one', which 'one' are we going to be? I certainly don't want to fade out as an individual—not to be 'me' any more. That makes marriage sound like a take-over bid! But perhaps it is not meant to be a take-over so much as a merger. A fusion of our lives, so that one person's weaknesses are compensated for by the other person's strengths; an adding-to rather than a taking-away, for both of us. Rather than cramping and confining us, perhaps this oneness is intended to bring a new dimension to our lives. For if we are secure in the certainty of each other's love and understanding, maybe we can enjoy a special kind of freedom. The freedom to fulfill our potential; to live life to the full in a way that we could never do alone.

A
GROWING
LOVE

Love is not the natural state
of our lives;
but selfishness, jealousy and indifference are...

Love comes as a gift;
love must be renewed constantly.

Love grows out of our experience with God;
love grows out of our acceptance of ourselves;
love grows out of our acceptance of each other.

Ulrich Schaffer

LOVE: A WAY OF LIFE

Love is patient and kind; it is not jealous or conceited or proud; love is not ill-mannered or selfish or irritable; love does not keep a record of wrongs; love is not happy with evil, but is happy with the truth. Love never gives up; and its faith, hope, and patience never fail.

Paul: from the New Testament

We love because God first loved us.

John: from the New Testament

Love is not a single act, but a climate in which we live, a lifetime venture in which we are always learning, discovering, growing.

It is not destroyed by a single failure, or won by a single caress.

Love is a climate—a climate of the heart.

Ardis Whitman

TODAY

If we knew that life would end tomorrow,
would we still waste today on our
quarrels? Would we fritter the precious
hours away, taking refuge behind that wall
of icy silence, creeping out only to hurl
another barrage of angry words—invisible
missiles, but in every way as deadly as
broken bricks or bottles?

If we knew that life would end tomorrow,
would we keep a tally of wrongs,
determined not to be the first one to give
in? Or would we cease to care who had
started it, knowing that no one is
completely in the right, and that in this
kind of war we shall both end up as losers?

If we knew that life would end tomorrow,
surely we would treasure today. Fill the
hours to the brim with love and laughter
instead of anger and bitterness, creating
jewel-bright memories which would
lighten our hearts instead of dark regrets
which could twist and destroy.

If we knew that life would end tomorrow. . .
but who can say that it will not? The only
time of which we can be certain is today.
So today I will reach out for your hand.
Today I will say 'I'm sorry' and 'I love you'.

FORGIVE AND FORGET

When a couple come to me and want to get married, I always ask them if they have once had a real quarrel—not just a casual difference of opinion, but a real fight.

Many times they will say: 'Oh no! Pastor, we love each other.'

Then I tell them: 'Quarrel first—and then I will marry you.'

The point is, of course, not the quarrelling, but the ability to be reconciled to each other. This ability must be trained and tested before marriage. Not sex, but rather this quarrel test, is, as I see it, a 'required' premarital experience.

The question is, therefore: Are we able to forgive each other and to give in to each other?

Walter Trobisch

There is no hope for happiness in harboring hurt feelings or thoughts. In marriage of all places we cannot live in the past. We must, if we are to be happy together, learn the discipline of forgiving and forgetting. In marriage we cannot allow ourselves to be chained to yesterday's mistake or last year's failure. Bridges must be burned, and with God's help they can be.

John Drescher

Be humble and gentle. Be patient with each other, making allowance for each other's faults because of your love. . . Don't let the sun go down with you still angry—get over it quickly. . . Quarrelling, harsh words, and dislike of others should have no place in your lives. Instead, be kind to each other, tenderhearted, forgiving one another, just as God has forgiven you. . .

Paul: from the New Testament

MAKING
THE BREAK

Dear Mom,

 I came home this afternoon—home for good! We had a quarrel and I went too far. Slammed out of the front door, and said I wasn't coming back. But you were out! Just as well really, because it gave me time on my own. Time to think about you and Dad. Did you ever threaten to leave us all and go back to Grandma? I can't imagine it! And then I thought about what you said to me on my wedding day. Do you remember?

 'There will always be a welcome here for you,' you said, 'and you can come back any time. But from now on your home is with your husband, and he must have the first place in your life. When you quarrel, I'll help you dry your tears, but I won't take sides. If there are problems that you both want to discuss, then we'll be glad to help, but I want no part in tale-telling or gossip!'

 You're right of course—though I wouldn't have admitted it an hour ago! Thank you for letting me enjoy the peace and order in your home. I've gone back now, to get things put to rights in mine.

A MARRIAGE FEAST

Fast from criticism and feast on praise,
Fast from self-pity and feast on joy,
Fast from ill-temper and feast on peace,
Fast from resentment and feast on contentment,
Fast from pride and feast on humility,
Fast from selfishness and feast on service,
Fast from fear and feast on faith.

THANK YOU

Thank you for the care you take
in making out of our house a home;
in creating out of our living room
more than just a good room—
        but a place in which my mind can be free,
can rest and be at ease...

Thank you
for the flowers on my desk,
for the mended sweater,
for the choice of music
with which you woke me...

Thank you for granting me silence.
Thank you for swallowing your words
when you noticed my inability
to deal with yet more information...

Thank you
for just taking over
when I couldn't any more;
when too much was just too much.

Thank you
for your patience,
allowing me to develop at my own speed.

Thank you
for sharing your fear, your joy,
your struggle, your love
and your life with me.

Ulrich Schaffer

ON BEING
A HUSBAND

Be faithful to your own wife
and give your love to her alone. . .
be happy with your wife
and find your joy in the girl you married. . .
Let her charms keep you happy;
let her surround you with her love.

The Book of Proverbs

Husbands, show the same kind of love
to your wives
as Christ showed to the church
when he died for her. . .
That is how husbands
should treat their wives,
loving them as part of themselves.
For since a man and his wife are now one,
a man is really doing himself a favour
and loving himself when he loves his wife.
No one hates his own body
but lovingly cares for it. . .
So . . . a man must love his wife
as a part of himself.

Paul: from the New Testament

MEMO TO MY WIFE

You asked me what I wanted for my birthday. Any gift from the list that follows would ensure that I'm the happiest of men:

1. Please greet me with a smile and a kiss when I come home, and act as if you're pleased to see me, even if it's been 'one of those days'.
2. Give me time. Time to make the mental switch from work to home at the end of the day. Time to potter, or even do nothing at all, without making helpful suggestions about the jobs awaiting my attention. Time to talk about the things that bother me and sometimes time to do nothing—except to be with you.
3. Please remember that often I would rather have you in my arms than in the kitchen baking my favorite cake.
4. When I make a suggestion, look for the possibilities rather than the difficulties.
5. Tell me my faults, if you must, but do it gently, and in private.
6. When I ask you to do something, please put it somewhere near the top of your list.
7. Let me know that I am still important to you, that you need me.
8. Say 'I love you'—and mean it—every day.
9. Smile!

ON BEING
A WIFE

A good wife is her husband's pride and joy.
She is worth more than precious gems!
Her husband can trust her,
and she will richly satisfy his needs.
She will not hinder him,
but help him all the days of her life. . .
She is a woman of strength and dignity,
and has no fear of old age.
When she speaks, her words are wise,
and kindness is the rule for everything she says.

The Book of Proverbs

Wives, fit in with your husband's plans . . .
Be beautiful inside, in your hearts,
with the lasting charm
of a gentle and quiet spirit
which is so precious to God.

Peter: from the New Testament

Allow your husband the privilege
of being just a man.
Don't expect him to read your mind,
or give you the security,
the joy, the peace, the love
that only God himself can give.

Ruth Bell Graham

THE GIFT OF WORDS

Thank you, God, for teaching us to talk to one another.
Thank you for the gift of words.
Thank you for giving us each other with whom to share our hopes, our fears, our problems and our plans.

Thank you for that assurance, that since there is no fear in love, we can be totally honest, completely ourselves, without the risk of ridicule or rejection.

Thank you for showing us the need to listen. To listen with our hearts as well as with our ears. To sense the needs that may remain unspoken beneath a torrent of words. And to know that when there are no words to meet the situation, then love can be a silent song—a touch that says 'I'm in this situation with you', a smile that reassures 'You're doing fine'.

Thank you that we have learned the need for patience. The discipline to talk things through until both minds are satisfied. Even if we then return to the original solution!
Thank you for teaching a talkative partner brevity, and a quieter one how to express himself.

Thank you, God, for teaching us to talk to one another.
Thank you for the gift of words.

INSIDE STORY

The Bible does not say very much
about homes;
it says a great deal
about the things that make them.
It speaks about life and love
and joy and peace and rest.
If we get a house and put these into it,
we shall have secured a home.

John Henry Jowett

WELCOME HOME

I thought that our house should be properly furnished before others could feel at home.

You said, 'Come any time', and when they did, sat them on the floor without a qualm. And the house *was* properly furnished—with people, with love and with laughter.

I thought that everyday food was for family only; that meals I could offer to guests must have hours of planning and preparation.

You said, 'It will be pot luck, but you're welcome to share what we have.' Then sandwiches in the garage while you worked on the car became a picnic, and baked beans around the kitchen-table a dinner-party.

I thought that overnight guests were rare creatures whose coming was a special event.

You said, 'We have an empty bed; stay as long as you need to.' And they took you at your word, so that our tiny spare bedroom with its bare boards and narrow bed is rarely empty for long.

I thought that our home was our castle.

You said, 'Let down the drawbridge. Having a home is a miracle to be shared.'

TAKE TIME

'Today we're going out!' you said. 'The jobs can wait. It's time we enjoyed ourselves.'

And so we pushed the washing back into the basket, closed the door on that half-decorated bedroom and left our work-a-day selves behind in the cupboard with the tool-box!

What made today so special? Wandering hand in hand through the quietness of the park? Laughing at the antics of the ducks as we scattered the remains of our lunch on the river? Finding that book we've always wanted at the back of the market-stall? Or was it just the sunshine that seemed to turn our world to gold?

Perhaps it was all of those things—and yet none of them. Today was special because we took time. Time to talk; time to find out what we were thinking and why; and time to remember that marriage may be hard work, but it's also intended to be fun!

ROOTS-AND WINGS

There are only two lasting things that we can give our children.
One is roots. The other is wings.

Our baby has received so many lovely gifts. And each one is a token of
the joyful welcome that exists for him. But there are things which he will
need that money cannot buy and loving hands can never manufacture.
Please show us, God, how we can give those precious but invisible gifts
to this new son of ours—roots and wings; security and freedom.

The books say that he'll need to feel secure, to know that we will
always love him, come what may. But we're just human beings—
beginners in the school of parenthood. There may be times when we
don't feel so loving, when daily living is just too 'daily' and the fabric of
our family life gets frayed around the edges. Give us your love then,
God; help us to know that if human parents get it wrong from time to
time, we can all depend completely on a heavenly Father who never
makes mistakes.

The freedom bit is harder. There are so many dangers all around
him. Our instinct is to mold and train, to shelter and protect. And this is
right. But in the midst of all our caring, he must be allowed to be
himself. To grow into the special person that you have planned for him
to be, not some pale copy of another. So, Lord God, help us to explore
your world together. Enable him to discover his own gifts and develop
them fully. And when we have done all that we can, give us courage to
stand aside and allow him to fly, knowing that your arms will always be
around him wherever he goes.

LEARNING
ABOUT LOVE

The most important thing a father can do for
his children is to love their mother.

Theodore Hesburgh

A child's most basic security is in knowing
that his parents love each other. It is even
more important than their love for him. He
feels assured of being part of a strong,
satisfying relationship and is certain that
he'll never be abandoned. . .

The only people who really know how
to express love are those who have seen love
expressed. A child knows his parents more
intimately, more honestly than anyone else
in his life. Therefore, what he is going to
learn about love will come from watching
them, day after day.

J. Allan Petersen

A PSALM FOR MARRIAGE

I am married, I am married,
and my heart is glad.
I will give thanks to the Lord
for the love and protection of my husband.
I will give thanks for the blessed protection
and satisfaction of my home.
I will give thanks that I have someone of my own
to help and comfort and even to worry about,
someone to encourage and love.
My husband is beside me
wherever I need to go.
My husband is behind me
supporting me in whatever I need to do.
I need not face the world alone.
I need not face my family alone.
I need face only myself and my God alone.
And this is good.
This is very good.
Whatever our differences,
whatever our trials,
I will give thanks to the Lord
for my husband and my marriage.

Marjorie Holmes

A WALLED GARDEN

My sweetheart, my bride, is a secret garden,
a walled garden, a private spring. . .

Song of Songs

'Your marriage,' he said, 'should have
within it, a secret and protected place, open
to you alone. Imagine it to be a walled
garden, entered by a door to which you only
hold the key. Within this garden you will
cease to be a mother, father, employee,
homemaker or any other of the roles which
you fulfill in daily life. Here you are
yourselves—two people who love each
other. Here you can concentrate on one
another's needs.'

And so we made our walled garden.
Time that was kept for us alone. At first we
went there often, enjoying each other's
company, sharing secrets, growing closer.
But now our days are packed with plans and
people. Conversation has become a message
scribbled on a pad. The door into our garden
is almost hidden by rank weeds of busy-
ness. We claim we have no time because we
have forgotten. Forgotten that love grows if
it is tended, and if neglected, dies. But we
can always make the time for what is most
important in our lives.

So take my hand and let us go back to
our garden. The time we spend together is
not wasted but invested. Invested in our
future and the nurture of our love.

THE GOOD DAYS OF MARRIAGE

Dear Lord, thank you for the good days of marriage. The days when we wake up pleased with each other, our jobs, our children, our home and ourselves.

Thank you for our communication—the times when we can really talk to each other; and the times when we understand each other without so much as a gesture or a word.

Thank you for our companionship—the times when we can work together at projects we both enjoy. Or work in our separate fields and yet have that sense of sharing that can only come when two people's lives have merged in so many other ways, so long. Thank you for our times of privacy. Our times of freedom. Our relaxed sense of personal trust. Thank you that we don't have to clutch and stifle each other, that we have learned to respect ourselves enough to respect the other's individuality.

Thank you, Lord, that despite the many storms of marriage we have reached these particular shores.

Marjorie Holmes

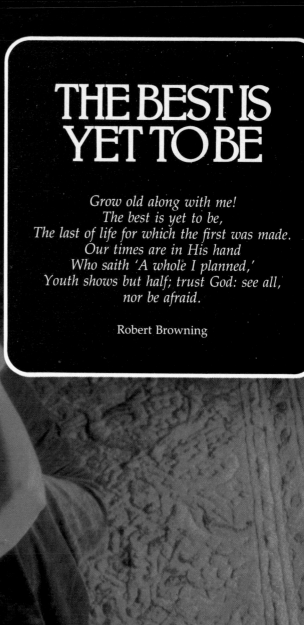

THE BEST IS YET TO BE

Grow old along with me!
The best is yet to be,
The last of life for which the first was made.
Our times are in His hand
Who saith 'A whole I planned,'
Youth shows but half; trust God: see all,
nor be afraid.

Robert Browning